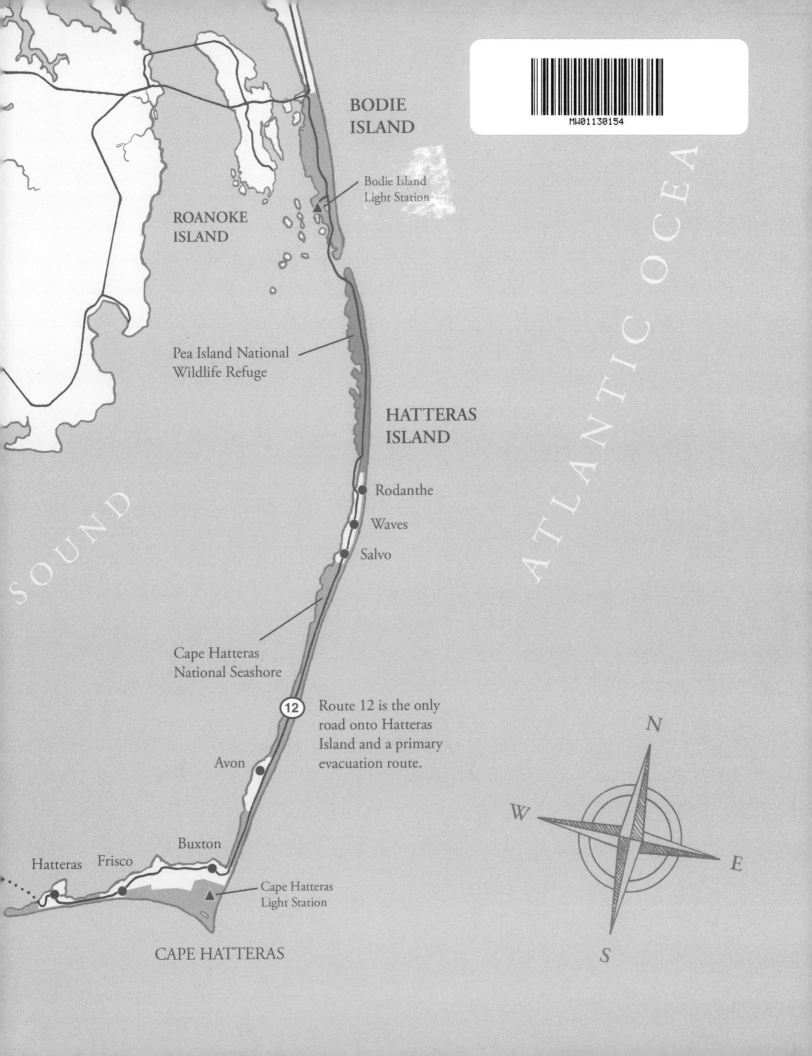

BODIE
ISLAND

Bodie Island
Light Station

ROANOKE
ISLAND

Pea Island National
Wildlife Refuge

HATTERAS
ISLAND

Rodanthe

Waves

Salvo

SOUND

Cape Hatteras
National Seashore

(12) Route 12 is the only
road onto Hatteras
Island and a primary
evacuation route.

Avon

Buxton

Hatteras   Frisco

Cape Hatteras
Light Station

CAPE HATTERAS

ATLANTIC OCEA

N

W   E

S

A storm is raging over the Atlantic Ocean.
Its terrible winds whip up waves taller
than houses. Torrents of rain pummel
the water's surface. Lightning and
thunder split the sky. A weather buoy
measures 85 miles-per-hour winds.

This is no ordinary storm.

This is a . . .

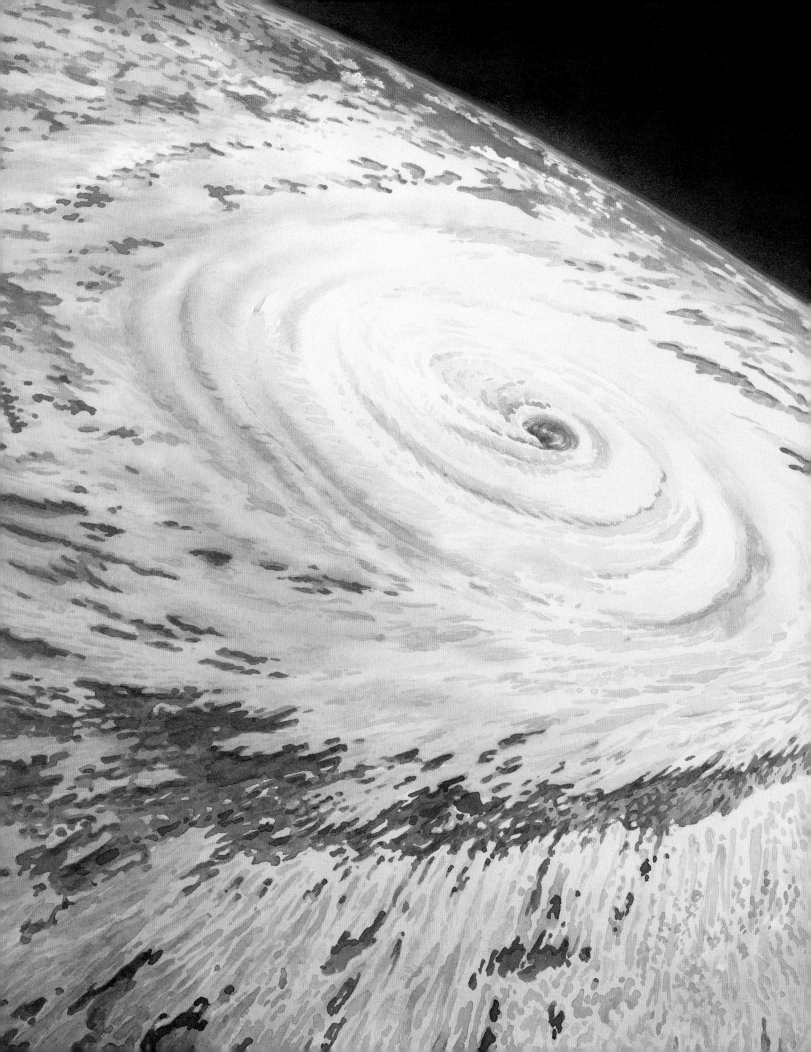

HURRICANE

Jason Chin

NEAL PORTER BOOKS

HOLIDAY HOUSE / NEW YORK

Hurricanes are large, rotating storms that form over the ocean. Once they get going, they can live for weeks and travel thousands of miles. If they reach land, their howling winds, raging waves, and torrential rains can cause terrible destruction. Hurricanes are the most powerful storms on Earth, and this one is heading toward North America.

Luckily it's being watched.

A weather satellite hovering more than 22,000 miles above our planet is taking pictures of the hurricane. It sends a new image of the storm back to Earth every minute.

GOES Weather Satellite
In addition to observing hurricanes, this satellite is used to monitor smoke, lightning, tornadoes, and even space weather.

Meteorologists at the National Hurricane Center in Miami, Florida, have been have been following this storm for days. They use satellite images to observe what the storm is doing and to create forecasts. Their forecasts tell people where the storm is and where it is going, and warn everyone who is in harm's way.

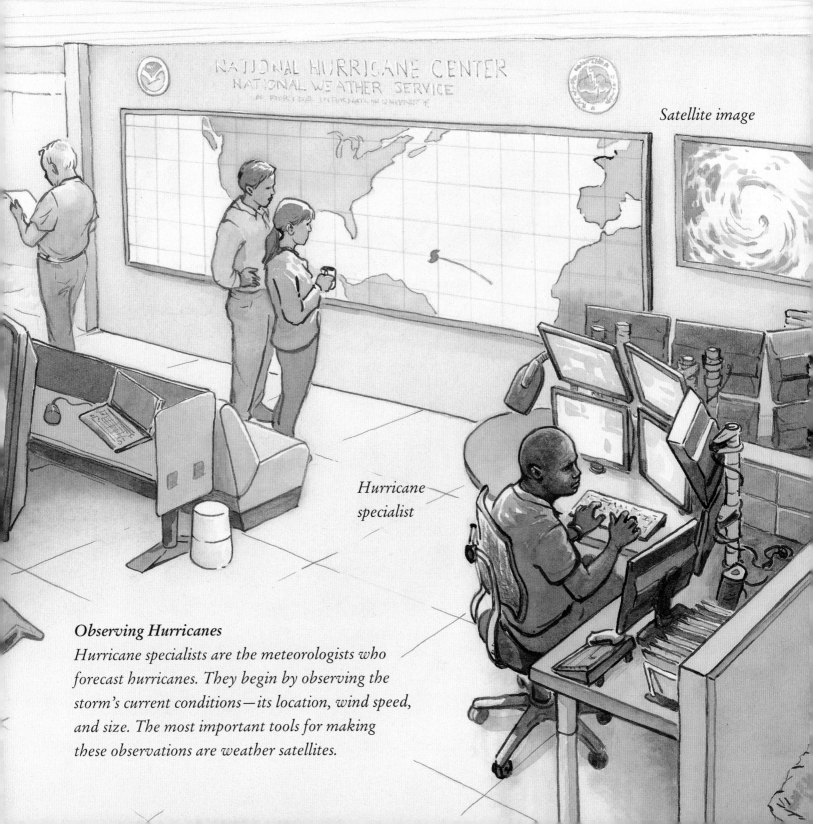

Satellite image

Hurricane specialist

Observing Hurricanes

Hurricane specialists are the meteorologists who forecast hurricanes. They begin by observing the storm's current conditions—its location, wind speed, and size. The most important tools for making these observations are weather satellites.

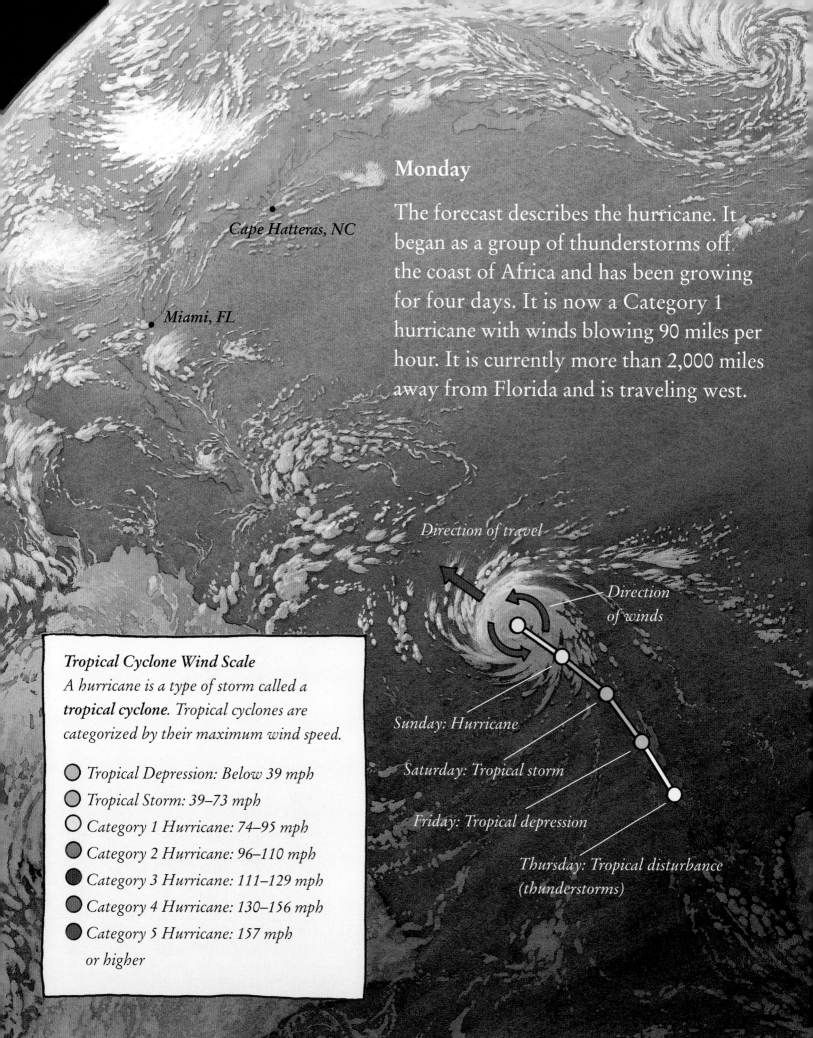

Monday

The forecast describes the hurricane. It began as a group of thunderstorms off the coast of Africa and has been growing for four days. It is now a Category 1 hurricane with winds blowing 90 miles per hour. It is currently more than 2,000 miles away from Florida and is traveling west.

Cape Hatteras, NC

Miami, FL

Direction of travel

Direction of winds

Sunday: Hurricane

Saturday: Tropical storm

Friday: Tropical depression

Thursday: Tropical disturbance (thunderstorms)

Tropical Cyclone Wind Scale
A hurricane is a type of storm called a **tropical cyclone.** *Tropical cyclones are categorized by their maximum wind speed.*

○ *Tropical Depression: Below 39 mph*
○ *Tropical Storm: 39–73 mph*
○ *Category 1 Hurricane: 74–95 mph*
○ *Category 2 Hurricane: 96–110 mph*
● *Category 3 Hurricane: 111–129 mph*
● *Category 4 Hurricane: 130–156 mph*
● *Category 5 Hurricane: 157 mph or higher*

People in coastal towns across the United States and the Caribbean pay attention to hurricane forecasts. On Hatteras Island, North Carolina, news of the storm spreads quickly.

People chat about it on the beach.

Kids talk about it at school.

Fishermen discuss it at the docks.

It isn't long before everyone on the island hears about the hurricane.

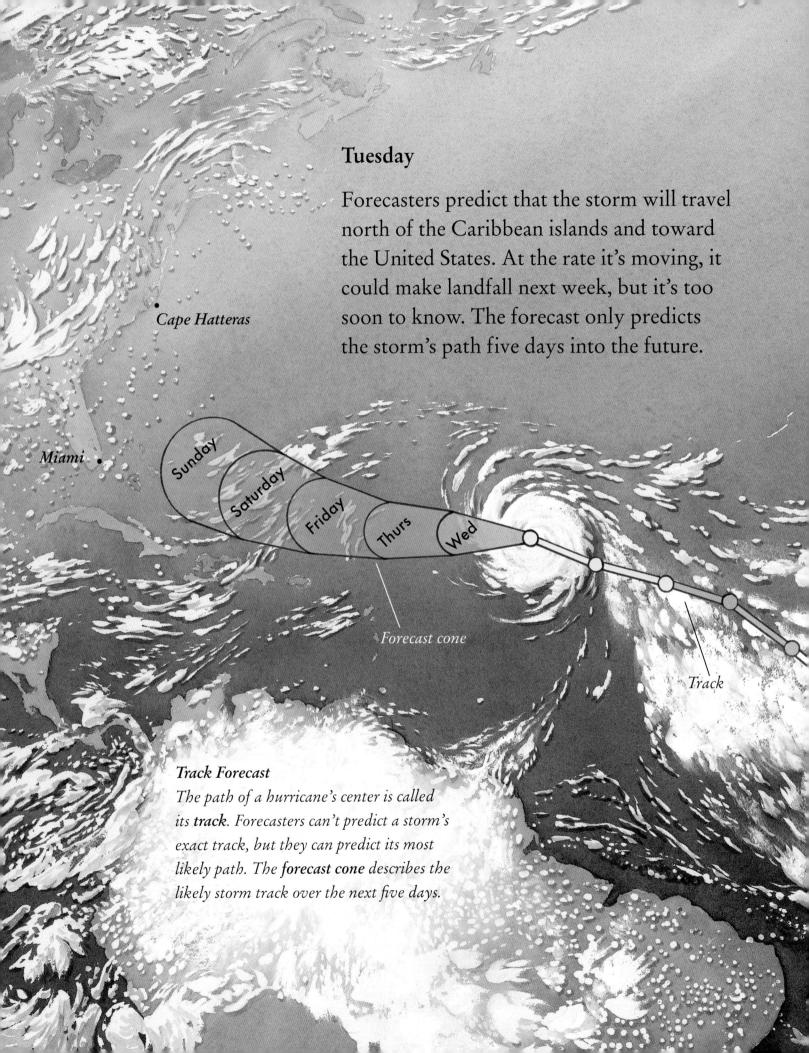

Tuesday

Forecasters predict that the storm will travel north of the Caribbean islands and toward the United States. At the rate it's moving, it could make landfall next week, but it's too soon to know. The forecast only predicts the storm's path five days into the future.

Cape Hatteras

Miami

Sunday

Saturday

Friday

Thurs

Wed

Forecast cone

Track

Track Forecast
*The path of a hurricane's center is called its **track**. Forecasters can't predict a storm's exact track, but they can predict its most likely path. The **forecast cone** describes the likely storm track over the next five days.*

The residents of Cape Hatteras aren't worried yet, but they know what hurricanes are capable of.

"Prepare for the worst and hope for the best," they say.

They have emergency supplies on hand . . .

Don't worry, if we're in danger we'll go to Grandma's house.

. . . and plans for staying safe.

Wednesday

At the National Hurricane Center, forecasters work night and day to predict the hurricane's track. To make a good prediction, they need good observations of the storm. Satellite photos tell them a lot, but measurements made inside the storm are more accurate. Luckily they have help from . . .

Forecast model tracks

Forecast Models
Forecast models are computer programs that help with forecasting. They begin with current measurements of the storm and calculate its future track and intensity. Hurricane specialists use many different models to help them make the official forecast.

. . . the Hurricane Hunters.

The Hurricane Hunters are an elite group of
scientists and pilots who fly into hurricanes
to find out exactly what they are doing. Their
plane is an airborne weather station with
advanced technology for observing
conditions inside the storm.

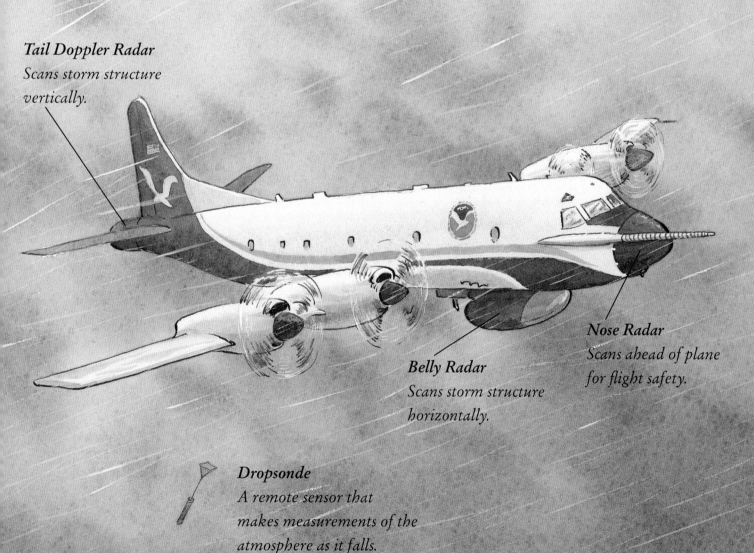

Tail Doppler Radar
Scans storm structure
vertically.

Nose Radar
Scans ahead of plane
for flight safety.

Belly Radar
Scans storm structure
horizontally.

Dropsonde
A remote sensor that
makes measurements of the
atmosphere as it falls.

National Oceanic and Atmospheric Administration (NOAA)
"Hurricane Hunters"

The navigator monitors the nose radar and plots the safest path through the storm.

The pilots and engineer keep the plane steady as it plows through the wind and rain.

A team of scientists operates the radar units, deploys the dropsondes, and sends the data they collect back to the National Hurricane Center.

The flight director oversees the mission and makes sure that the team collects all the information they need.

After spending five hours inside the storm, they finally head home. On their way out, they pass the next team on their way in. Multiple hurricane hunter crews will fly in and out of this storm continuously until it's over. It is a dangerous job, but they are proud to do it.

U.S. Air Force 53rd Weather Reconnaissance Squadron
"Hurricane Hunters"

Thursday

On today's mission, the Hurricane Hunters discover that the storm has become much more powerful. Hurricanes get their energy from warm ocean water, and this storm has been moving over *very* warm water. Its fastest winds have reached 115 miles per hour, making it a *major* Category 3 hurricane.

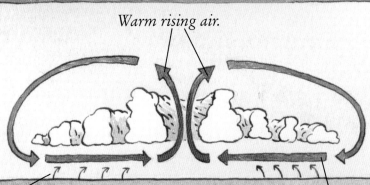

Warm rising air.

Warm ocean water heats the air above it.

Wind at the surface.

Warm Water Is Hurricane Fuel
When warm water heats the air above it, the warmed air rises. Surrounding air rushes in behind it, creating wind. The wind is warmed by the ocean, causing it to rise, too. The warmer the ocean, the faster the air rises and the faster the wind blows.

On Cape Hatteras, residents keep their cars fueled up, in case they have to leave quickly . . .

. . . they make sure their generators are working, in case the power goes out . . .

My generator won't start, can you take a look?

Of course.

. . . and they are always ready to help their neighbors.

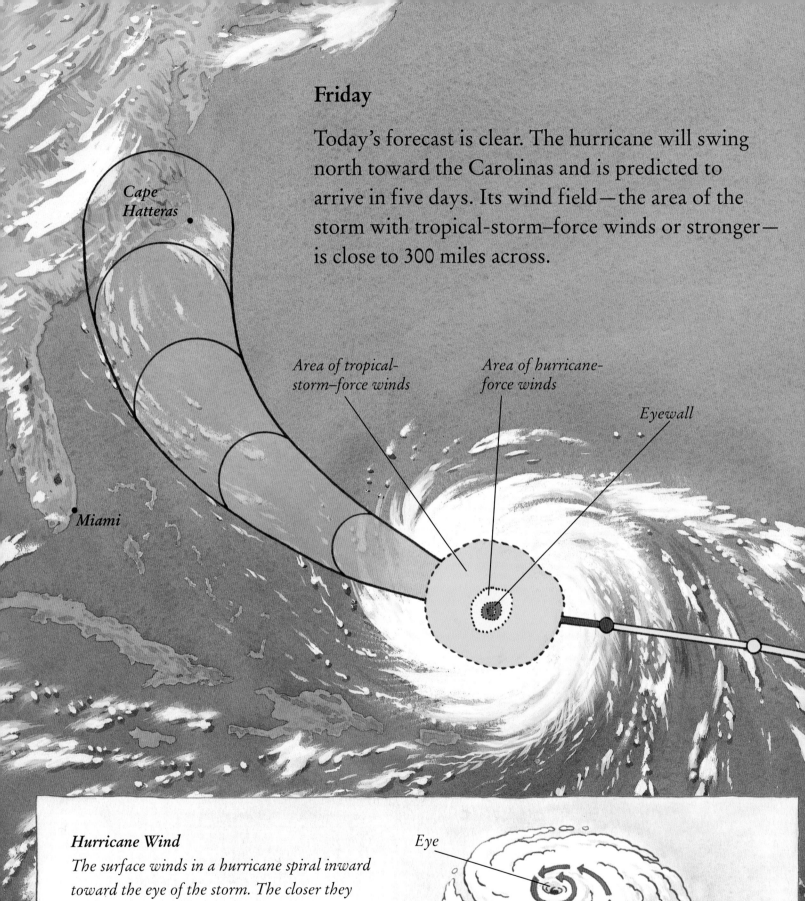

Friday

Today's forecast is clear. The hurricane will swing north toward the Carolinas and is predicted to arrive in five days. Its wind field—the area of the storm with tropical-storm–force winds or stronger— is close to 300 miles across.

Cape Hatteras

Miami

Area of tropical-storm–force winds

Area of hurricane-force winds

Eyewall

Hurricane Wind

The surface winds in a hurricane spiral inward toward the eye of the storm. The closer they get, the faster they blow. The fastest winds are in the eyewall, just outside the eye.

Eye

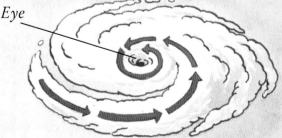

Now that they know the storm is heading their way, the residents of Cape Hatteras rush to prepare. They clean up their yards and tie down anything that can't be brought inside. The powerful wind could turn any loose objects into dangerous flying missiles.

They board up windows
to protect the glass from
flying objects . . .

. . . pull small boats
out of the water to
keep them safe . . .

I'm heading to the store.
Do you need anything?

I could use more
bottled water, thanks!

. . . and they check in
with their neighbors.

The grocery store is busy with residents stocking up on food and water. They'll need it if they are stranded on the island.

Cape
Hatteras

Miami

Saturday

The storm is now four days away and it's pushing a bulge of water ahead of it called a storm surge. When the surge reaches land, forecasters predict that the sea will rise 6 feet or more, causing dangerous flooding.

Storm Surge
A hurricane pushes a bulge of water ahead of it, called a storm surge.

Storm surge

Land that is normally dry . . .

Normal high tide

. . . is flooded by the storm surge.

10 foot storm surge

On the island, large boats
are tied down with extra rope,
so they don't wash away . . .

. . . and cars are moved
to higher ground in case
the island floods.

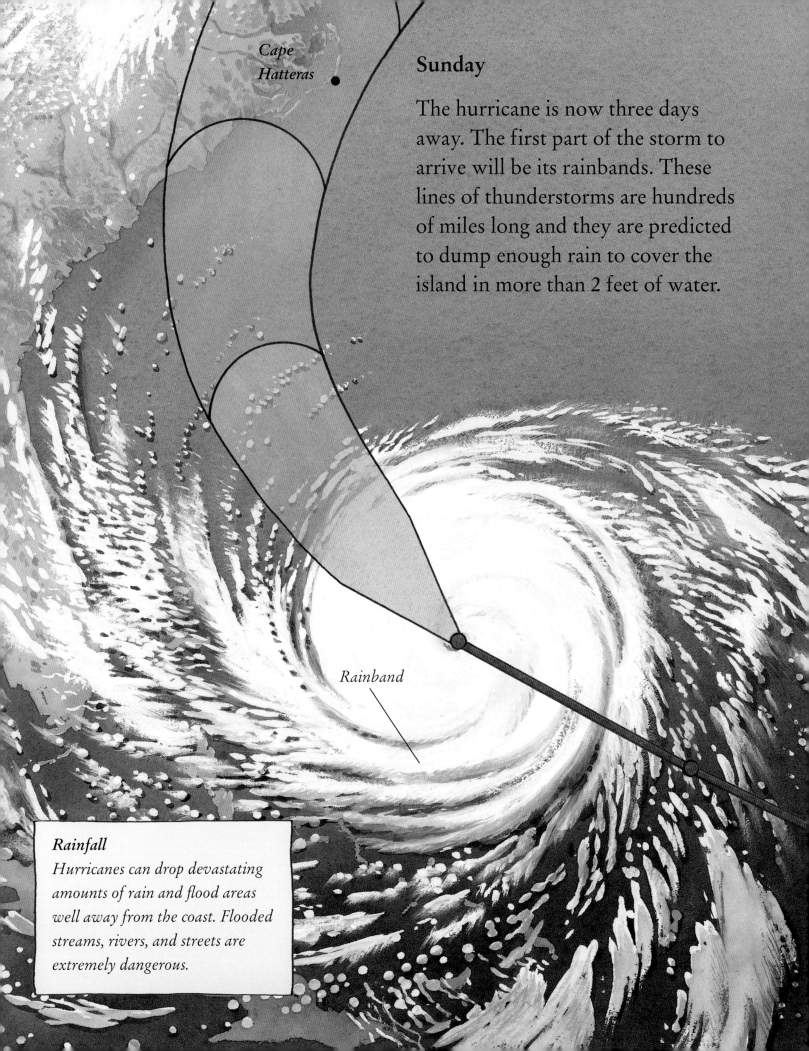

Cape Hatteras

Sunday

The hurricane is now three days away. The first part of the storm to arrive will be its rainbands. These lines of thunderstorms are hundreds of miles long and they are predicted to dump enough rain to cover the island in more than 2 feet of water.

Rainband

Rainfall
Hurricanes can drop devastating amounts of rain and flood areas well away from the coast. Flooded streams, rivers, and streets are extremely dangerous.

The hurricane is likely to knock out power, block roads, and cut off the island. People's lives will be at risk, so an evacuation is ordered. Residents check on their neighbors one last time.

Then they lock the doors and windows to keep them from blowing in . . .

and leave.

Cape Hatteras

Hurricane Watch
*A hurricane watch is issued
for areas where hurricane
conditions are possible
within forty-eight hours.*

Monday

The storm has encountered cooler water and is beginning to weaken. Forecasters predict that it will make landfall as a Category 1 storm, but as it weakens its wind field could grow larger. A hurricane watch is issued for towns up and down the coast.

Tuesday

This is the last chance to evacuate before it becomes too dangerous to travel. The hurricane's wind field is now more than 300 miles across. Strong gusts of wind have reached the island and waves are crashing against the dunes. A hurricane warning is issued for the island.

The hurricane will arrive tomorrow.

Hurricane Warning
A hurricane warning is issued
for areas where hurricane conditions
are likely within thirty-six hours.

Wednesday

As the hurricane's outer bands reach the island, gusts of wind rattle road signs and the rain begins to fall in sheets.

Soon the wind is howling, accompanied by a barrage of thunder and lightning. Ocean swells spill over the dunes.

Hours pass and the wind continues to get stronger, becoming a high screaming whistle. Branches snap. The power goes out.

The storm has been over the island for eight hours. Rain is not falling down anymore; it's blowing sideways. Broken branches slam into houses. Shingles *POP* as they are ripped from rooftops. The island is in the eyewall. Then suddenly . . .

. . . it is calm.

There is barely a breeze and the air is hot and humid. The island is in the eye of the storm, but this moment of calm is deceiving. The storm is only half over and just as quickly as it left . . .

. . . the storm comes back.

On this side of the eye, the wind blows in the opposite
direction and water comes rushing in from the west.
There are no dunes to protect this side of the island
and the water rises fast.

Boats strain on their ropes as waves crash into the docks.

Finally, in the early hours of the morning the rain slows to a drizzle and the wind is merely gusty. The worst is over.

Thursday

On Cape Hatteras the sun is shining and the sky is clear. The hurricane has moved on, but the damage has been done.

The highway is covered in sand and water, and no one can return until it has been cleared. Crews from the highway department and electric company are already hard at work.

Friday

When the residents can finally return home, they find the island in tatters. Many streets are still flooded and the power is still out.

Buildings have been damaged, debris is everywhere . . .

. . . and the docks are wrecked.

But it could have
been worse. Boarded-up
windows weren't broken. Cars on
high ground didn't flood. The residents
have food and water and generators for power.

Most important of all, everyone survived. Now, the
residents will begin the long task of cleaning up . . .

. . . and they will get through it together.

Can I borrow your chain saw?

Hurricane Structure

Hurricanes have a central area of low pressure called the eye. The winds in the storm spiral inward toward the eye. They speed up as they get closer, and carry lines of thunderstorms called rainbands with them. A towering vortex of rain and wind called the eyewall surrounds the eye. The strongest winds in the storm are found in the eyewall, but the eye itself is calm.

Hurricane Season

Most hurricanes develop in the late summer and fall when ocean waters are at their warmest. In the North Atlantic, hurricane season lasts from June to November with September seeing the most hurricanes. In the southern hemisphere, cyclone season is roughly the opposite, beginning in November and running through April.

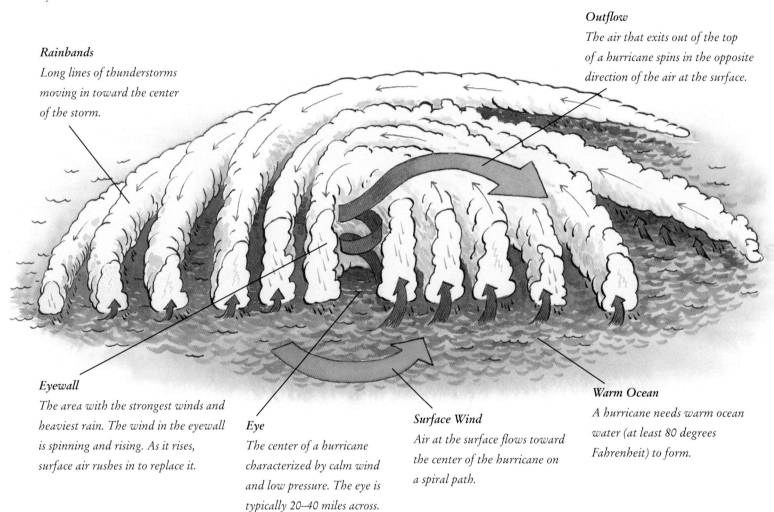

Outflow
The air that exits out of the top of a hurricane spins in the opposite direction of the air at the surface.

Rainbands
Long lines of thunderstorms moving in toward the center of the storm.

Eyewall
The area with the strongest winds and heaviest rain. The wind in the eyewall is spinning and rising. As it rises, surface air rushes in to replace it.

Eye
The center of a hurricane characterized by calm wind and low pressure. The eye is typically 20–40 miles across.

Surface Wind
Air at the surface flows toward the center of the hurricane on a spiral path.

Warm Ocean
A hurricane needs warm ocean water (at least 80 degrees Fahrenheit) to form.

Tropical Cyclones Around the World

Tropical cyclones are rotating storms that form over tropical oceans around the world, and a hurricane is a strong tropical cyclone. Strong tropical cyclones are given different names depending on where they originate. In the North Atlantic and eastern North Pacific, they are called **hurricanes**. In the western North Pacific they are called **typhoons** and in the South Pacific and Indian oceans they are called **cyclones**.

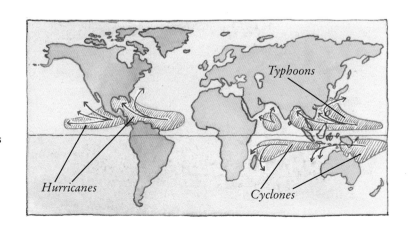

Hurricane Formation

Tropical cyclones begin as an area of stormy weather called a **tropical disturbance**. Warm water evaporates and heats the air above it, causing the air to rise and form clouds and thunderstorms. An area of *low pressure* forms at the surface.

The surrounding air blows in toward the low pressure. The wind follows a curved path, and the storm clouds start to rotate. When there is clear rotation, the system becomes a **tropical depression**, the weakest form of a **tropical cyclone**.

As the wind spirals in, it is warmed by the ocean and it rises faster, making the pressure drop further. The lower the pressure, the faster the wind blows. When it reaches 39 miles per hour, the system becomes a **tropical storm**.

As the ocean keeps warming the air, the pressure drops lower, and the wind blows faster. When it reaches 74 miles per hour, the storm becomes a Category 1 **hurricane**.

The End of the Storm

Tropical cyclones need certain conditions to form and to keep going. They need warm ocean water that is at least 80 degrees Fahrenheit. If a storm loses its source of warm water (if it moves over land, for example) it will weaken and dissipate. Other necessary conditions are moist air and calm winds around the storm. Dry air and strong winds called **wind shear** can cause a hurricane to decay.

Why Do Hurricanes Spin?

As a hurricane's winds flow inward, the rotation of the Earth causes them to curve. This is what makes hurricanes spin, and it's known as the Coriolis effect. Hurricanes always spin counter-clockwise in the Northern Hemisphere and clockwise in the Southern Hemisphere.

Saffir-Simpson Hurricane Wind Scale

Hurricanes are categorized by their maximum sustained wind speed. Hurricanes reaching Category 3 strength or greater are major hurricanes.

Category 1: 74–95 mph
Category 2: 96–110 mph
Category 3 (major): 111–129 mph
Category 4 (major): 130–156 mph
Category 5 (major): 157 mph or greater

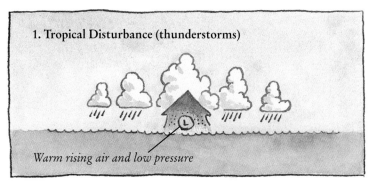

1. Tropical Disturbance (thunderstorms)

Warm rising air and low pressure

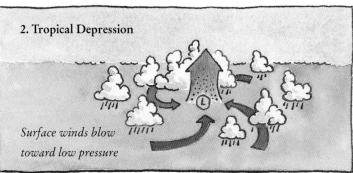

2. Tropical Depression

Surface winds blow toward low pressure

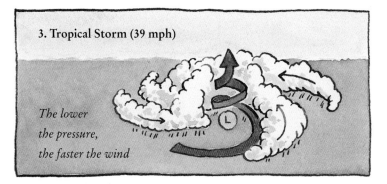

3. Tropical Storm (39 mph)

The lower the pressure, the faster the wind

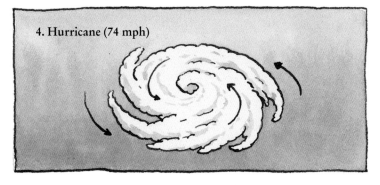

4. Hurricane (74 mph)

Why Do Hurricanes Travel?

A hurricane's track is determined by the large-scale winds that surround it, called the *steering flow*. These winds carry the hurricane along, similar to a leaf floating in a stream. Hurricanes typically move from east to west and away from the equator (north in the northern hemisphere, and south in the southern hemisphere).

Meteorology: The Science of Earth's Atmosphere

Meteorologists are scientists who study Earth's atmosphere and how it behaves. There are many kinds of meteorologists. Some do research to better understand how the atmosphere works, while others work on forecasting the weather. Hurricane specialists at the National Hurricane Center are experts in hurricane forecasting. Their job is critical to warning coastal communities about approaching hurricanes and saving lives.

Observing Hurricanes

The first step in forecasting a hurricane is to observe the storm's current conditions—its pressure, wind speed, location, and size. Storm observations come from satellites, weather buoys, sail drones, ships, land-based radar, and reconnaissance flights. Satellites are the forecaster's most important tool for observing a storm because they are always watching. Forecasters use the satellite images to estimate the conditions in the storm, but when a storm becomes a threat to land, more accurate measurements are needed. These are made by the Hurricane Hunters.

The Hurricane Hunters

There are two groups of Hurricane Hunters in the United States: the *U.S. Air Force Reserve 53rd Reconnaissance Squadron* and the *National Oceanic and Atmospheric Administration (NOAA) Hurricane Hunters.* Both fly into hurricanes to gather data for forecasts, but NOAA crews primarily fly scientific research missions. Together, these brave pilots and scientists have dramatically improved our understanding of hurricanes and our ability to forecast them.

Hurricane Forecast Models

After observations of the hurricane are made, the data are added to computer programs called *forecast models*. The models are run on powerful supercomputers and calculate where the hurricane will go and how strong it will become. Different models make different predictions and meteorologists look at many models to help them make their forecast.

The Forecast

Using computer models for guidance, hurricane specialists create the forecast. The forecast shows where the hurricane is and predicts its future track, size, and intensity. Forecasters also make rainfall and storm surge predictions and issue hurricane watches and warnings. It is impossible to predict exactly what will happen, so the forecast describes what is most likely to happen.

Naming Hurricanes

The storm in this book is unnamed because it is fictional, but real tropical cyclones are given human names (such as Irene) when they become tropical storms. The World Meteorological Organization maintains lists of names in alphabetical order. The first storm of the season receives the name starting with the letter *A*, the second storm is given the name starting with *B,* and so on. When a storm is particularly destructive, its name is permanently retired from the list.

Hurricane Dangers

When they make landfall, hurricanes are capable of terrible destruction and, worst of all, they can be deadly. Hurricanes are categorized by their wind speed, but the category doesn't describe all of a storm's dangers. In fact, the deadliest part of the storm is the water, not the wind. To stay safe, people in hurricane-prone areas must prepare for all the dangers that hurricanes can bring.

Storm Surge Flooding

As a hurricane approaches land, it piles up water ahead of it in a bulge called a storm surge. The surge can raise sea level by 20 feet or more, causing catastrophic and deadly flooding.

Freshwater Flooding

A hurricane's torrential rainfall can cause major flooding and erosion. Saturated land can collapse in landslides, and rivers and streams can jump their banks. Freshwater flooding is extremely hazardous.

Wind

Hurricanes produce some of the strongest winds on the planet. High winds can destroy buildings and literally blow people off their feet. Any loose material—branches, roof shingles, broken glass—can become deadly projectiles in hurricane force winds.

Tornadoes

As if a hurricane's wind wasn't enough, most hurricanes also spawn tornadoes. Thankfully, the tornadoes associated with hurricanes tend to be weak (for a tornado) and short lived.

Climate Change and Hurricanes

The Earth's oceans and atmosphere are getting warmer because of human activity, mainly the burning of fossil fuels. Unfortunately, hurricanes are predicted to be more dangerous in a warmer world. There is evidence that this is already happening, and the atmosphere is still getting hotter.

Rising Seas, Higher Storm Surge

Sea level is rising as the ocean warms, which will make storm surge flooding worse because storms are moving over higher seas to begin with.

Hotter Oceans, Stronger Storms

Warmer oceans have more heat available to power hurricanes, so hurricanes are expected to grow stronger.

Hotter Air, More Rain

Warmer air can hold more moisture than cooler air, and hurricanes are expected to drop more rain as the atmosphere heats up. In certain regions, hurricanes are already bringing more rain.

Many Unanswered Questions

Hurricanes are very complicated, and scientists have a lot of questions about how they will change in the future. Will the overall number of hurricanes go up or down in a warmer world? (Studies suggest the number could go down *slightly*.) Will they intensify faster? (Recent studies suggest that they will.) Will they move more slowly? How will hurricanes change in different regions? Meteorologists around the world are working to answer these questions and more to improve hurricane forecasts and keep people safe.

Further Reading

Simon, Seymour. *Hurricanes*. Smithsonian/Collins, New York, 2007.

Rocco, John. *Hurricane*. Little, Brown, New York, 2021.

Cherrix, Amy. *Eye of the Storm: NASA, Drones, and the Race to Crack the Hurricane Code (Scientists in the Field)*. Clarion, New York, 2017.

The National Hurricane Center: https://www.nhc.noaa.gov

NOAA/AOML Hurricane Research Division: https://www.aoml.noaa.gov/hurricane-research-division/

NOAA Hurricane Hunters: https://www.omao.noaa.gov/omao/noaa-hurricane-hunters

Air Force Hurricane Hunters: https://www.403wg.afrc.af.mil/About/Fact-Sheets/Display/Article/192529/53rd-weather-reconnaissance-squadron-hurricane-hunters/

NASA Space Place: Hurricanes: https://spaceplace.nasa.gov/hurricanes/

Selected Sources

Shonk, Jon. *Introducing Meteorology: A Guide to Weather*. Dunedin, London, 2013.

Ahrens, C. Donald. *Essentials of Meteorology: An Invitation to the Atmosphere*, 7th ed. Cengage Learning, Stamford, CT, 2014.

Knowlton, C. W., et al. *Hurricanes: Science and Society*. University of Rhode Island Graduate School of Oceanography. Kingston, RI, 2014.

Laing, Arlene and Jenni-Louise Evans. *Introduction to Tropical Meteorology*, 2nd ed. The COMET Program and National Center for Atmospheric Research. 2016. Accessed online 11/28/23 at: https://www.meted.ucar.edu/tropical/textbook_2nd_edition/index.htm.

A Note from the Author

This book is my attempt to capture all sides of a landfalling hurricane, from the science of tropical cyclones and hurricane forecasting, to the impact on a coastal community. The story is set on Hatteras Island—commonly called Cape Hatteras—one of several barrier islands off the coast of North Carolina. The islands' location puts them in the path of many Atlantic hurricanes. Over the past century, more than thirty hurricanes passed close to Cape Hatteras—roughly one every three years. Sure enough, my research trip to Hatteras for this book in 2023 was delayed by Tropical Storm Ophelia.

The fictional hurricane in this book is based on several storms that impacted Cape Hatteras in recent years, including Isabel (2003), Dorian (2019), and one that affected both Hatteras and my home state of Vermont: Irene (2011).

Like the storm in this book, Irene originated in the Atlantic. After impacting Puerto Rico, Hispaniola, and the Bahamas, it reached the U.S. mainland near Cape Hatteras. It walloped Hatteras Island with a storm surge topping 10 feet, damaging homes and cutting a channel clear through the island, but Irene wasn't finished. It continued to damage communities on its way north, eventually reaching New England as a tropical storm. In Vermont, its devastating rainfall flooded towns, destroyed houses, and damaged more than two thousand roads. In both Hatteras and Vermont, the recovery was long and costly. The official National Hurricane Center report determined that Irene caused forty-eight deaths in total and cost 15.8 billion dollars in damages in the U.S. alone.

Unfortunately, global warming, caused primarily by burning of fossil fuels, is making hurricanes more dangerous. As the global temperature rises, we are likely to see wetter, more powerful, and more destructive hurricanes. As I write this, communities across the U.S. and Caribbean are reeling from Hurricane Beryl (2024). Fueled by record-high ocean temperatures, Beryl rapidly intensified to become the earliest Category 5 storm in Atlantic hurricane history. It ravaged several Caribbean islands before making landfall in Mexico and then Texas. When the remnants of the storm reached Vermont, they brought torrential rains that destroyed roads, flooded homes, and killed two people. The higher the global temperature rises, the more likely extreme storms like Beryl will become.

Although hurricanes can be terribly destructive, it is possible to stay safe with good preparation, adequate resources, and early warning. For that we rely on the scientists who study and predict the weather. From the hurricane researchers to the hurricane hunters, from the satellite engineers to the weather forecasters, there are thousands of people working together to better predict extreme weather and keep us safe. The more I learned as I worked on this book, the more impressed and grateful I became. The efforts of the meteorological community often go underappreciated, but the work they do is becoming more and more important as the world warms, and to my mind they are heroes.

Acknowledgments

I would like to thank the residents of Hatteras Island for sharing their hurricane stories, many of which made their way into this book. Over the course of our communications, I heard repeatedly about the importance of helping neighbors through hurricanes and their aftermath. This sentiment was echoed by people from other hurricane-prone regions, too. It seems that the worst weather on Earth often brings out the best in humanity. The generous spirit of the Hatteras community is something I will not forget. I am particularly grateful to the teachers and students at Cape Hatteras Elementary.

A number of experts shared their knowledge with me and they also have my thanks. This book wouldn't have been possible with out the generosity of:

John Cangialosi, Hurricane Specialist, National Hurricane Center
James Done, Project Scientist, National Center for Atmospheric Research
Michael McGuire, Director at The Hatteras Island Community Emergency Response Team (CERT)
Shirley Murillo, Acting Director of the Hurricane Research Division, NOAA/AOML
Drew Pearson, Director of Emergency Management, Dare County, North Carolina
Jonathan Shannon, Public Affairs Specialist, NOAA Aircraft Operations Center
Maria Torres, Communications / Public Affairs Officer, National Hurricane Center
Ping Zhu, Professor in the Department of Earth and Environment at Florida International University

Dedicated to Matthew, Catherine, and Anne and to the memory of Andy McKinney

Neal Porter Books
An imprint of Holiday House Publishing, Inc.

Text and illustrations copyright © 2025 by Jason Chin
All Rights Reserved
HOLIDAY HOUSE is registered in the U.S. Patent and Trademark Office.
Printed and bound in January 2025 at Toppan Leefung, DongGuan, China.
The artwork for this book was created using pen and ink, watercolor, and gouache on Saunders Waterford paper.
Book design by Jennifer Browne and Jason Chin
www.holidayhouse.com
First Edition
10 9 8 7 6 5 4 3 2 1
Library of Congress Cataloging-in-Publication Data

Names: Chin, Jason, 1978– author.
Title: Hurricane / Jason Chin.
Description: First edition. | New York : Neal Porter Book, Holiday House, [2025] | Includes bibliographical references. | Audience: Ages 4–8 | Audience: Grades K–1 | Summary: "The community of Hatteras Island, North Carolina prepares to weather a category three hurricane, aided by cutting-edge science"— Provided by publisher.
Identifiers: LCCN 2024017349 | ISBN 9780823458493 (hardcover)
Subjects: LCSH: Hurricanes—North Carolina—Cape Hatteras—Juvenile literature.
Classification: LCC QC944.2 .C495 2025 | DDC 551.55/2091821—dc23/eng/20240516
LC record available at https://lccn.loc.gov/2024017349

ISBN: 978-0-8234-5849-3 (hardcover)

EU Authorized Representative: HackettFlynn Ltd, 36 Cloch Choirneal, Balrothery, Co. Dublin, K32 C942, Ireland. EU@walkerpublishinggroup.com

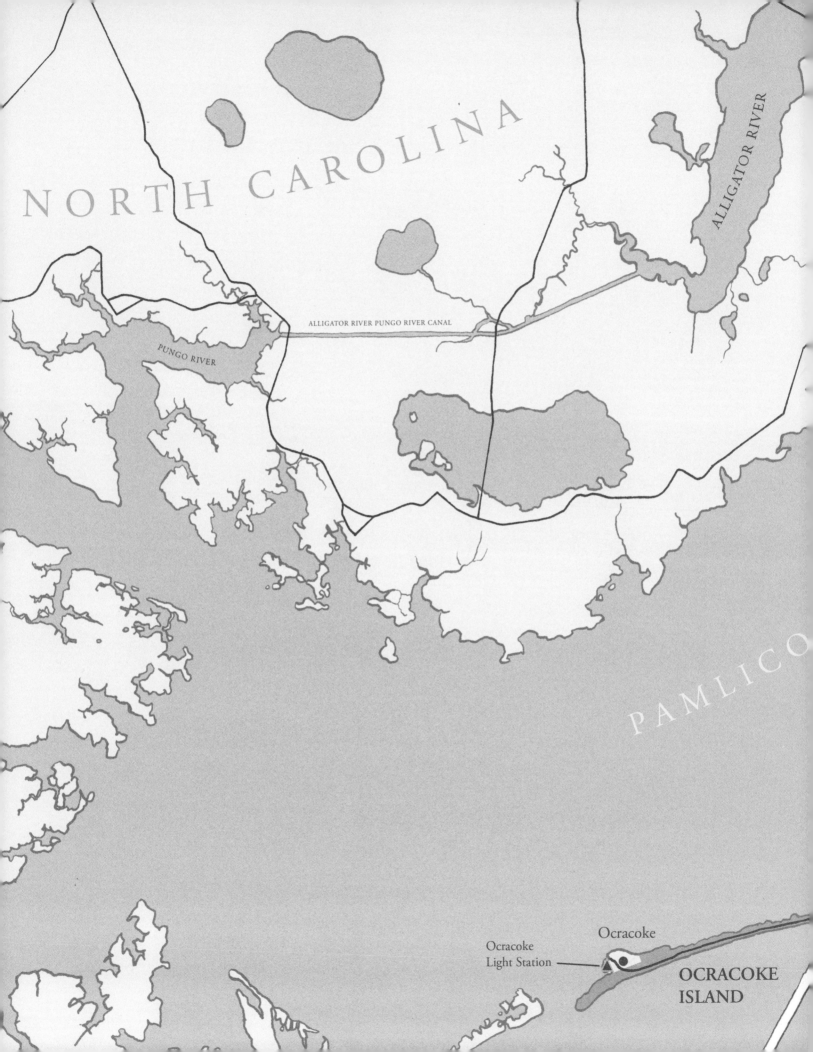

NORTH CAROLINA

ALLIGATOR RIVER

ALLIGATOR RIVER PUNGO RIVER CANAL

PUNGO RIVER

PAMLICO

Ocracoke

Ocracoke
Light Station

OCRACOKE
ISLAND